AWFUL ALVIN
and Other Peculiar Poems

Stephen Brooke

Arachis Press 2015

AP

Awful Alvin and Other Peculiar Poems

©2015 Stephen Brooke

ISBN 978-1-937745-23-3

Arachis Press
4803 Peanut Road
Graceville, FL 32440
http://arachispress.com

Awful Alvin

Some children are as good as gold,
As sweet as sugar, I am told;
Like little angels, some will say,
But Alvin never was that way.

He was the naughtiest of boys;
Sometimes he broke his sister's toys.
He even scribbled on the wall,
For Alvin wasn't nice at all.

He was so bad that others came
To call him by a different name;
"There's Awful Alvin," they'd all say
And none of them would want to play.

AWFUL ALVIN ~ 4

No, Alvin wouldn't do as told,
Not even when his mom would scold.
It didn't help to take time out;
He'd make an ugly face and pout.

His father told him, "When you're bad
It makes your mother and me sad."
But Alvin didn't seem to care;
He threw a tantrum, then and there!

What this boy needed was a friend,
A somebody who would depend
On Alvin to watch out for him,
To be his pal through thick and thin.

His parents loved him and they knew
A boy without a friend won't do,
So, just as Alvin's birthday neared,
A large, mysterious box appeared.

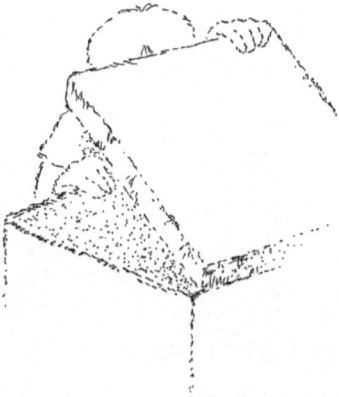

Who knows what might be in a box?
It could be toys, it could be socks!
Then from inside, there came a yip;
He had it open in a zip.

It was a puppy, Alvin's own,
To care for and to give a home,
To be his friend in every way
And stay at his side, come what may.

But even this small pup could see
A boy named "Awful" might not be
The kind of friend a puppy needed;
Poor Alvin knelt down and he pleaded.

"Will you be my friend? If you would,
I'll try my hardest to be good,"
He promised and he didn't lie;
The best that we can do is try.

The dog believed him, too, I guess;
He wagged his tail and that meant yes.
Then into Alvin's arms he wriggled
And licked his face until he giggled!

From that day, Alvin did his best
To show the pup he'd pass the test
And so, at last, he found a friend;
His story has a happy end.

For Alvin was okay, inside,
And proved that when he really tried
He could be better than before;
He's not so awful anymore.

Watch Out!

Clumsy cat,
watch out for that!
Get down from there!
I do declare,
every time
you choose to climb,
something breaks.
Make no mistakes,
you little vandal,
I can handle
your innocent look—
you're an open book.
You'd better know
that out you go
if things don't change,
if you rearrange
my shelves again.
Are you listenin'?
Hey, not the vase!
That sweet little face
won't save you now;
I don't know how
You get away
not having to pay

for each misdeed.
You think you need
but climb in my lap,
to purr and to nap
without one regret
and I'll just forget?
It's true, I guess,
but look at the mess
you've made, you cat!
Watch out for that!
Clumsy cat,
watch out—oh, drat!

Spin Offs

If the world spins around,
Why don't I slide out of bed?
Should I wear a safety belt
To avoid bumps on my head?

If the world spins around,
Walking west should be quite fast;
Every time I lift my feet
Earth would just go zooming past.

If the world spins around,
Shouldn't everyone feel sick?
I get dizzy when I spin;
Very dizzy, very quick!

Amelia the Chameleon

Amelia the chameleon
couldn't decide on a hue;
so she wouldn't be seen, she tried out green,
though yellow or tan should do.

She wished to be bold, not just the same old,
she wanted something new,
and Amelia the chameleon
then grew so sad she turned blue!

The King Must Sing

A call from the Great, Grand High Frog
brought all, to the least polliwog,
before his throne, high on a log,
for he was the King of the Bog.

The King blinked his big, bulging eyes,
announcing, to each frog's surprise,
"I'm tired of just catching flies
or sitting up here looking wise.

"It's time that I act like a king,
and I know exactly the thing:
a leader's voice surely should ring,
so someone must teach me to sing!"

No, frogs cannot actually frown,
but some of their mouths did turn down;
they even asked, "What's with this clown?
His head is too big for his crown!"

For this task appealed to no one,
with most frogs preferring to shun
all work and just sit in the sun—
they're lazy sorts, when all is done.

One little tad finally spoke,
"Your Highness must certainly joke.
You already have a fine croak
and don't need the help of we folk."

"Oh yes," all agreed eagerly,
"You must set your royal voice free!"
and puffed him up with flattery,
so now the King sings constantly.

They soon recognized their mistake—
his bellowing made the swamp shake;
it wavered and often would break.
All night long he kept them awake.

They raised no more hale froggy cheers,
they cried in their cold froggy beers,
for his singing quickly brought tears
to frog eyes and even frog ears.

He wheezed like a broken down bus,
it couldn't be more hideous,
and led to a great froggy fuss.
Why, some even started to cuss!

But what can one do but just sigh
and live with what comes of a lie?
The Great, Grand High Frog sings on high—
the other frogs? They must get by!

The Really Deep Hole

Out by the fence, in their back yard,
Young Lynn and Pete were trying hard
To peek inside a hole they'd found,
A little hole dug in the ground.

Lynn said, "I wonder what lives here
And if it could be somewhere near."
"Perhaps," Pete answered, "there might be
Some mice, but it's too dark to see."

Then asked her, as he took a peep,
"Do you think it is really deep?"
Lynn told him, "No, I don't think so
But then with holes, you never know.

"I guess it's too big for a mole,
So maybe it's the kind of hole
Where rabbits or a tortoise stay
And only goes a little way."

"Don't be so certain that it's nice,
I bet there's more down there than mice;
Things that would give you the shakes,"
Warned Petey, "even worse than snakes.

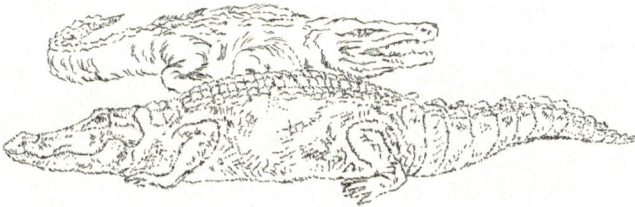

"There could be rivers underground
Where alligators float around,
Just waiting for us to fall in!"
"I don't like that at all," said Lynn,

"But I think elves might have a mine
That's deep down where the sun can't shine,
With diamonds there so big and bright
They don't need any other light."

"Okay," said Pete, "then further down,
Dinosaurs can still be found."
"Well, at least their bones are there,"
Lynn answered, trying to be fair.

"And far below," continued Pete,
"We would go on until we meet
A dragon with a pile of gold,
In a cave that's dark and cold.

"If we were quiet, we could creep
By that old dragon in his sleep."
"What if he wakes up?"asked Lynn.
"We're breakfast," said Pete, with a grin.

"A really deep hole will run right
On through earth to the other side,
But that's too far to go today,"
Said Lynn, "and still have time to play."

"Let's come back when it's not so late,"
Suggested Pete, and Lynn said, "Great,
It should be here; I think that such
A really deep hole won't move much."

They know it's fun when we pretend
That really deep holes never end
And guess about what lives way down
Miles and miles beneath the ground.

If we imagine things that might
Be hidden somewhere, out of sight,
Like Lynn and Pete and look ourselves,
We may find rabbits or find elves!

Role Call

Sometimes he is an alien,
Who thinks I'm good to munch,
And grabs me with long tentacles,
Still sticky from his lunch.
He wraps them tight around my waist
He starts to squeeze and crunch;
Then I will have to pry them loose,
That icky, sticky bunch!

He'll be a lawman, sure to shoot
If I resist arrest;
I fall right down and kick my legs,
I try to die my best.
But he may not be certain, so,
He tickles, just to test!
Whatever else my brother is,
He always is a pest.

Pretty Kitty

There was an itty-bitty pretty kitty
Who lived in an apartment in the city;
She looked out of her window every day
And told herself "I ought to run away!"

For right across the street there was a park
She thought the perfect place to have a lark;
"If I go there I'm sure that I shall find
Trees to climb and rocks to hide behind!

"And there in wait I patiently would lie
Until a butterfly should flutter by.
Then I'd leap out and catch it in my paws!
Why? Oh, I'm a cat, so just because."

It seems she truly had become quite bored
By all her kitten toys and she ignored
Enticement by stuffed mice and balls of yarn.
The pretty kitty didn't give a darn!

So, through an open door the kitty slipped
And down the flight of stairs she gaily skipped;
Well, cats may not exactly skip, it's true,
Still, she bounced off to see all that was new.

She planted both her itty-bitty feet
When she reached the busy, bustling street;
There she sat and watched the cars whiz by
And wondered whether she should even try.

"Oh no," she thought, "I could end up quite flat
And that is no condition for a cat!"
But right across the road lay all that grass—
The kitty waited for the cars to pass

And made a wild dash for the other side.
It's fortunate the street was not too wide!
Though her little heart beat double-time
The sights spread out before her seemed sublime.

But as she set out to explore the park,
Suddenly a dog began to bark;
Then another and soon there were three
Joining in canine cacophony.

It was too much; she turned around and ran
Through the traffic, right in front of a van!
As fast as four legs can, she climbed the stairs,
Dashed through the door and hid behind the chairs.

"This is where I belong, right here at home!"
The kitty thought, and vowed to never roam.
"Why, here I'll find no terrible mishaps
Just hands to smooth my fur and pleasant naps."

The itty-bitty pretty kitty purred
But later on that night she rose and stirred—
Gazed through the window, out into the dark
And planned her next excursion to the park.

Three Little Poems

I did a deed, indeed I did,
I did a deed, as I was bid;
I did the deed with all due speed
And once I did it, ran and hid!

I laugh out loud, allowed to laugh,
I laugh out loud, though it's a gaffe;
I laugh aloud for I am proud
That when I laugh it's not by half!

I lent a loan, alone I lent;
I lent a loan and it was spent.
I lent the loan and now I moan
For what I lent was my last cent.

Fairy Tailing

I slip into the garden,
butterfly net in hand;
I aim to nab a fairy
for this is Fairy Land.

She may hide in the roses,
protected by the thorn,
and she will giggle gaily
to see me scratched and torn.

Or high in the magnolia,
she may alight and tease
me in my clumsy efforts
to net the evening breeze.

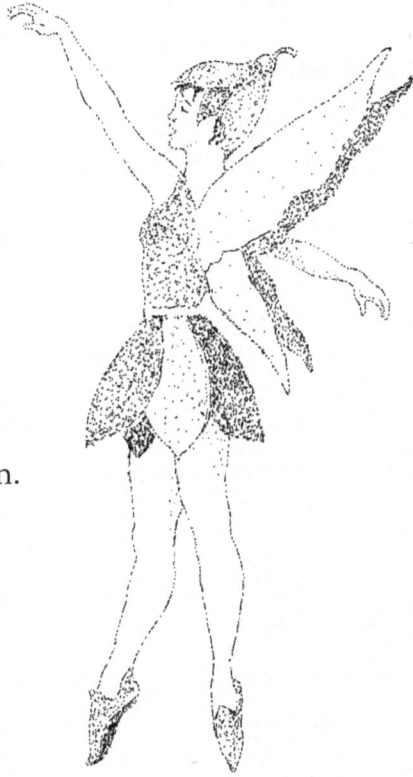

I'll catch that fairy someday
and hold her in my heart,
but only when she lets me;
I've known that from the start.

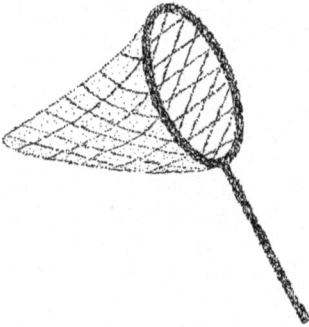

The Grumpy Old Man

Down a way, across the street,
lives the grumpiest old man.
He grumbles at his neighbors' kids
and at his neighbors, when he can.

Visitors are never welcome,
I can tell when I walk by.
His gate is always closed and locked,
His fence is very, very high.

Let me be, is all he asks,
But I can imagine that
it must be lonely living with
no wife, no kids, no dog nor cat.

We don't like him very much,
though we might if he would let us.
Since no one ever bothers him
he can't say that he's truly met us.

Would it be okay to call him,
if I promised not to shout,
but asked politely, at his door,
Please, would you like to come out?

Maybe it would make no difference,
maybe he would stay inside,
but how could we know his answer
if nobody ever tried?

Someday, I'll go lots of places,
make friends with everyone I meet;
I'd like to start with the grumpy old man,
down a way, across the street.

Double Cross

Why did the chicken cross the road?
To reach the other side.
What did she do when she got there?
She hitched herself a ride.

Why did that chicken cross the road?
Why leave her native nest?
She'd been invited to my home
To be a dinner guest.

A chicken should not cross the road,
I'm certain that she knew,
When she arrived here, just to find
We're serving chicken stew.

Squirrely

Each little boy squirrel
needs a squirrel girl;
she'll make his tail curl,

preferably.
They'd sit in a tree
and act squirrely,

going nuts together
and not caring whether
birds of a feather

can be furry.
There's too much hurry
and squirrels don't worry

anyway.
They chase and play,
They swing and sway

on branches high
and sometimes try
to actually fly

or at least they hop
to another tree-top.
They chatter non-stop

as squirrels do
and so would you
if a squirrel too!

An Anole

An anole
is an annoying animal—
though green when first seen,
stick around and it's bound
to turn brown.

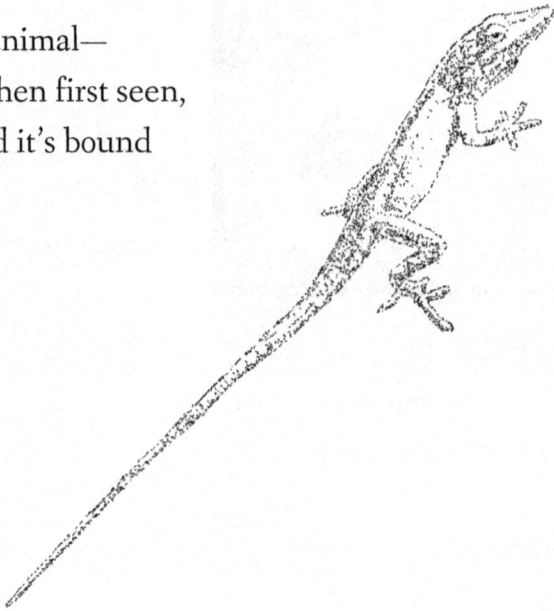

Cobbler

I am a gobbler
of peach cobbler,
with ice cream laid on thickly.
I can't resist
Nor do I desist;
It disappears quite quickly!

A golden crust
is a must,
with fruit that's sweet and ripe;
bite after bite,
if it's done right
you'll hear not a single gripe!

The cobbler beckons,
I do want seconds—
I can't resist that aroma.
But if I ate
another plate
I'd go into a coma.

The Explorers

Jeffy and Jason went exploring
Through a jungle full of roaring;
Down a secret path they filed
Deep in the deepest darkest wild.

Until they reached a hidden pool,
Filled with water, clear and cool.
There, beneath the tall trees' shade
Is where the whoppapotamus played.

The boys were just a little scared
But Jeffy got as close as he dared
To such a whopper of a 'potamus,
For he's braver than a lot of us.

"We're looking for our brother Pat;
Can you tell us where he's at?"
That's not good grammar, I agree,
But then Jeffy's only three.

The beast gave out a mighty yawn,
Then stretched upon the grassy lawn.
"I think I've seen the boy," he said,
"Does he have freckles and hair that's red?"

Jason spoke now, feeling bolder,
As well he should, since he's older.
After all, he's nearly six,
But wary of whoppapotamus tricks.

"That must be our Pat, for sure.
Please tell us where to find him, sir.
If you don't, I'll hold my breath
And so will little brother Jeff!"

"I wouldn't want you turning blue
So let me tell you what to do.
Close your eyes and count to ten—
Patrick will appear, right then."

Now Jason counts to ten with ease
Though Jeff has trouble after his threes
And doesn't like to close his eyes
When whoppapotami are near by.

But Jason wouldn't hear his "can'ts"
And said they ought to take a chance
The whoppapotamus was nice.
Still, Jeffy did peek once or twice.

And though the boys might have been rash,
On reaching ten they heard a splash.
It was Pat, they couldn't be wrong,
He'd been in the water all along.

They played and swam with their new friend,
Yet even the best of fun must end
For three little boys on a day so fine.
Their mommy's calling, it's nap time.

Then Jeff said "Thank you very much
Mister Whoppapotamus.
We'll be back, so don't you cry
But now we have to say goodbye."

Jeffy and Jason and Pat had to go,
Up that jungle path they know.
I'm sure they'll come to play again—
Tomorrow, if it doesn't rain!

Thank you for reading this little collection of poems. I hope you have enjoyed them. ~*Stephen Brooke*

Stephen Brooke is an author and artist. He lives in an old farmhouse in the Florida Panhandle with his kitty, Miss Molly Meow.

More books by Stephen Brooke are available from the Arachis Press.
http://arachispress.com

www.ingramcontent.com/pod-product-compliance
Lightning Source LLC
Chambersburg PA
CBHW021922040426
42448CB00007B/872